Writing Your Heritage:
A Sequence of Thinking, Reading, and Writing Assignments

Writing Your Heritage:
A Sequence of Thinking, Reading, and Writing Assignments

Deborah Dixon

Berkeley
National Writing Project
1993

National Writing Project, Graduate School of Education,
615 University Hall, University of California,
Berkeley, CA 94720.
Telephone 510-642-0963
Fax 510-642-4545

Writing Teachers at Work #1
Series editor: Miriam Ylvisaker

Cover design: Dennis Teutschel

Foreword

I want to offer two sets of observations or tell two different kinds of stories about the significance of Deborah Dixon's contribution to the National Writing Project's monograph series, "Writing Teachers At Work." My first set of observations will trace the intellectual and pedagogical provenience of the ideas and teaching strategies presented in the following pages and point to the significance of this book and "The Heritage Project" as a contribution to our collective expertise as a professional community of teachers of writing. My next set of observations tell a different kind of story about how this book got written — an emblematic story, ending provisionally with the publication of this book and illustrating through this particular case how the National Writing Project model of professional development characteristically transforms the professional lives of teachers.

The first story, the story about the ideas advanced in this book, begins with the dissatisfactions that Deborah felt in her first years of teaching college Freshman English courses as a graduate teaching assistant and as an instructor in a community college and in a university. In both settings she saw that the kinds of writing assignments she had been advised to use in her courses were not likely to help her students learn how to do the kinds of thinking and writing that would enable them to perform successfully in their subsequent college careers. It seemed to her, in fact, that the standard assignments she had been expected to give actually encouraged

— if they did not reward — perfunctory and conventional thinking and dull, relatively uncritical elaborations of standard ideas. Often the assignments seemed to elicit superficial thinking and logically incoherent writing.

Her observations of her own students — most of whom happened to be Mexican-Americans, African-Americans, or Asian-Americans — suggested not that her students lacked thinking skills or academically acceptable ways of organizing and presenting their thoughts, but that they more essentially lacked a commitment to the topics or ideas they were dealing with, and lacked as well the kind of intimate familiarity with their subjects that we ordinarily take for granted in any writer who would presume to present work to a reader.

Trusting her experience and her intuitions as a teacher and as a writer, Deborah started several years ago to experiment with some new writing assignments to replace the set of standard academic writing assignments she had previously felt obliged to use. Her experiments eventually became a carefully constructed sequence of assignments (that she would later call "The Heritage Project") that had three powerful instructional virtues. First, the sequence insured that students would be researching and writing about subjects in which they were personally invested and to which they were therefore likely to attend with serious, engaged, and concentrated thought. Second, the sequence was designed to build and draw upon funds of knowledge which would allow the students to move in steps to increasingly more demanding kinds of discourse — topics and ways of approaching topics that were increasingly more abstract and complex and that led authentically to the kinds of reflective and analytical discourse we associate with college-level writing. Finally, the sequence of tasks was designed to encourage and fit into a classroom structure that called for the sharing of finished pieces of writing as well as work in progress — a structure and sequence that fostered the development of the classroom as a model of a learning community, a community of readers and writers whose members inquire into common or similar problems and can benefit from sharing findings and methods. In designing such a sequence of assignments and in creating such a classroom structure, Deborah was intuitively building for her students the kind of intellectual and social framework that fosters and sustains research and writing in most academic fields or professions. It is also the kind of framework or learning community that Deborah was to find for herself in the Writing Project.

And this brings me to the second story I want to tell about the genesis of this book, one that traces the history of its composition from its first conception as a set of ideas to be shared with colleagues (and in the root sense of the word, "published" or made public) to a provisional ending with its publication by the National Writing Project. This story begins with a conversation Deborah and I had at the time of her interview as a candidate for a fellowship for our South Coast Writing Project Summer Invitational Institute in Composition, when I asked her what she did in her teaching that she believed in and that could provide the basis for a "hands-on" presentation that might be useful to her Institute colleagues. Our discussions of individual teaching strategies and promising lessons eventually led us to what Deborah believed in most of all, but that seemed to her not suitable for a presentation — her sequence of writing assignments in which students explored dimensions of their personal and ethnic heritage in the context of American cultural history.

As we discussed what Deborah actually did from week to week in her classrooms and what features characterized exemplary Writing Project presentations, she came to realize that the sequence of assignments she so much believed in could serve as the basis of a strong presentation if three conditions could obtain: 1) if she could select segments of some writing assignments to demonstrate by having her colleagues do the writing in the Institute within the compass of a 75-minute presentation; 2) if she could provide a coherent theoretical framework that would serve as a rationale for the assignment sequence and allow teachers to distinguish between the essential elements of such assignments and those elements that might be altered without subverting the purposes of the whole sequence; and 3) if she could provide models of student performance which would illustrate and support her theory and her practice. If she could do all of this and do it convincingly, I suggested encouragingly, she might also have the basis for a promising professional publication.

These conditions became the focus of Deborah's attention over the next several weeks as she planned her presentation and consulted with me and our Project co-directors in our role as coaches. By the time of our Institute orientation meeting several weeks later, but still a month before our Institute was to begin, Deborah had found a rationale for her project that used Moffett's discourse theory, and she had accumulated a promising collection of sample student work. By the time she made her presentation in our Institute some seven weeks later, Deborah had all the pieces in place and offered one of the most memorable presentations of the summer, one that any Writing Project site director would call exemplary. By that time, having read a number of teacher research reports and other articles by classroom practitioners and having spent a couple of weeks immersed in her own writing, Deborah was also already intrigued by the possibility of turning her well-received presentation into something more broadly publishable.

Following her presentation, I encouraged Deborah once again to think about publication for a wider audience and provided her with a possible model of the kind of piece she might write in the form of some volumes from the earlier "Writing Teachers at Work" series published by the National Writing Project. I also told her of the expectation among members of the National Writing Project Advisory Board that the NWP would soon resume publishing volumes in that series or in a similar format. That encouragement, along with the enthusiastic response of her Summer Institute colleagues to her presentation and the ongoing support of her Summer Institute writing group (which continued to meet monthly beyond the Institute and still meets now) was enough to set Deborah to work on what was to become the manuscript for this book.

Deborah showed me an early draft of a completed manuscript for my response within six months of completing the Institute. My response — quite aside from my appreciation for the pedagogical value of her manuscript — included astonishment that with her more-than-full-time teaching schedule (she was teaching five sections of Freshman English that semester) on top of her traditional responsibilities as a wife and mother she still managed to complete a thoughtfully conceived and well-written book manuscript in what seemed to me record time. When Deborah presented me with a substantially revised version of her manuscript I read it with delight and then forwarded it with confidence to NWP, where it was accepted for publication.

This second story about the transformation of one teacher's classroom practice into a book for a professional community is emblematic in the sense that it represents a more general story about how the Writing

Project works to honor and produce professional knowledge from the bottom up — from individual classroom practitioners to the profession at large. At a more personal level it is also emblematic as a story about how the Writing Project transforms the professional lives of individual teachers. Deborah's entry into the professional community of the Writing Project called upon her to construct a presentation for her colleagues which occasioned the transformation of her practical ideas for solving a problem in her own class into a strategy for teaching that could be presented to other practitioners in the context of a theory about the development of writers and supported by well-selected samples of student writing.

Not until Deborah was interviewed as a candidate for a Writing Project fellowship with its requirement that she offer a presentation on her own teaching practice to colleagues did she find herself in a professional context that called upon her to extend herself beyond her already established role as an expert classroom practitioner to that of both an expert and reflective practitioner and a producer of professional knowledge in her field. Never before had she found herself in a context in which her own teaching practice was to become the focus of her teaching in a presentation which would require her to articulate and reflect systematically on the principles behind her demonstrated practice. Although the step taken that day, during the interview, may not have represented a giant step for a thoughtful teacher like Deborah to make, it does mark the beginning of a major shift in the nature of her professional life and in her relationship to her daily work as a classroom teacher and as member of a profession. In that sense her story is the story of what the Writing Project is about and why teacher presentations are a seminal piece of the Writing Project professional development model.

Sheridan Blau, Director
South Coast Writing Project
University of California, Santa Barbara

Contents

Heritage is not some little trinkets that one gets from one's great-grandmother. Nor is it material possessions that one gets from a will. Heritage is physical traits, mannerisms, attitudes, tastes, and customs that people inherit from past generations.
—My Le

INTRODUCTION

I want to share with you the results of three years of thinking, trying, rethinking, and trying again with an assignment sequence in which I have attempted to address the personal as well as the academic needs of my students at the University of California at Santa Barbara. I teach in the Program of Intensive English, a program created to serve the needs of EOP students. They include African-Americans, Asian-Americans, Native Americans, Hispanics, and Caucasians. Their career plans are as varied as their backgrounds: engineering, medicine, teaching, art, marine biology, and so on. They share an eagerness to learn and a tolerance for hard work; they value a college education as a key to their futures. Although they are students at a four-year university, they still are in many cases unprepared to read sophisticated texts or analyze and synthesize ideas presented in their classes. Often they are the first in their families to attend college. Furthermore, many are bilingual or bidialectical, so they lack fluency in written English. For this reason, most view writing as an onerous task. My goal is to nurture a love of reading and writing through assignments that build skills and leave room for the joy that learning can and should provide.

The writing sequence that I've developed for my freshmen combines reading, short writing exercises, and journal entries, plus individual and group activities that culminate in a series of essay assignments. This series focuses on the heritage and backgrounds of students, and takes them from "Noting Down," journal writings; through "Looking Back," personal recollection and family stories; through "Looking Into," research projects and research papers; to "Thinking Through," the thesis essay.

I have structured my curriculum so that each assignment builds not only on preceding exercises and essay assignments, but also anticipates those that follow. It includes an introduction to the student's notebook that synthesizes all that has been discussed, written, and experienced. The sequence is structured so that my students *do* something, *read* something, *write* something, then pull it all together in a formal essay assignment. Each new assignment, whether informal or formal, uses the skills and the information generated in the assignments that came before: personal recollection leads to narration; the research assignment enriches that personal story; this same research informs the analysis that follows; the final synthesis pulls together all the material, all the skills, as well as evoking a reflection on the entire process.

Evolution of Sequence

A writing sequence can evolve quite naturally in ways suggested by James Moffett in his occasional paper entitled "Bridges: From Personal Writing To the Formal Essay" (No. 9, Center for the Study of Writing, University of California, Berkeley, Carnegie Mellon University, March 1989). Moffett calls "Noting Down" (journal, diary, logs) the basis of all student writing. From the journal, students move easily into "recollection" (autobiography and/or memoir). To help the students cross over from personal writing to cognitive writing (personal essay, thesis essay), Moffett suggests two avenues: through imaginative writing (fiction, plays, poetry) or through investigation (profile, case study, biography, factual article). In my work with students during the heritage sequence it has become clear to me that Moffett is quite correct in saying that "reportage and research represent an important bridge between personal writing and transpersonal writing" (4).

I have found this sequence to be useful not only at the university level, but also at the community college and high school levels. In fact, with some adjustments in the reading assignments, a high school teacher has taught this sequence successfully in her ESL classes. Portions of the

2

sequence have been taught, too, in seventh and eighth grades. In this paper I will tell you what I do and how I respond. I will share the composition and teaching theories that inform my teaching methods and my assignments. Here is a description of the process — the prewriting activities, the readings, and the essay assignments — along with examples from the work of students in my freshmen composition classes at UC, Santa Barbara.

PHASE I: Defining Heritage

We begin the process of defining heritage the first day of class. Before I ask students to write on the subject, I give them an opportunity to think on paper by diagramming their family tree. While I give them an outline to guide them, it is not important that they fill in every line. This is really a brainstorming session. As they create their trees, students write in not only whatever they know of names, places, and dates, but also occupations, religions, and important events, for this will jog their memories of family stories and traditions. To encourage them to participate fully, I demonstrate first with my own family tree, telling stories about my family and its history. Students follow this model; on Andrew's family tree, for example, his entries often become little character sketches. His grandfather is "Tyler: major diplomat during late thirties-fifties," and his grandmother is "Ruthie, Tyler's dutiful wife." An African-American student adopted by white parents, his blended family caused him some problems at first, since he thought he really didn't have a heritage. His views changed over the course of the term and he was able to complete all the exercises and writing assignments successfully. In fact, Andrew's initial dilemma seemed to add a tension that enriched his thinking and writing.

The students' first writing assignment springs out of this family tree. The assignment begins with a journal "freewriting":

> Choose one of your ancestors and write a letter or
> a tribute to him or her.

These freewrites take ten to fifteen minutes of class time. Typically, I write with my students and read aloud my tribute or letter as they do. By trusting them with my stories and my feelings, I give them reason to trust me and each other.

Hal,

You are courage. You did all that you did for others. The act of being a doctor in itself is challenging, but you took it a step further. Helping less fortunate people in all types of cultures, you were the best. Even now, years after your death, your name lives on. As your great-grandson, I am hopefull and fearfull at the same time. Hopefull that I might come close to your greatness, and fearfull that I will not. How could I even try. You risked your life to save others. Facing disease and feman with pride and daring, only to emerge victorious. You were the best of all adventurers, and stubornest of all humanitarians. You were and are still a legend of your time.
— Andrew

My Mother

Her hands are rough from working all her life. But they are still quick and lively as she move around the house doing her chores from morning to night. She was born in Canton, China. Her parents moved to Vietnam when she was a child. She grew up in Saigon, Vietnam. Her father started a business, selling flours. Being the oldest, she had to take care of her brothers and sister. She also had to help her mother with chores in the house. When she was twenty, she got married. Unlike other women, she get to see her husband before they got married. After she got married, she moved to Vung Tan, Vietnam, where her husband lived. — My Le

Tribute to My Great-grandfather

I don't know of any historical or 'great' event in which my great-grandfather participated. I however, believe that he was a great hero. He was my hero. He did not fight in a war

or save my life or any of those characteristics that you would usually attribute to a hero, but he was a great man. His name was Antonio Maciel Ceja and because of his love, strength, and strong will, he will always have a very special place in my heart. He will always be remembered and if it is God's will, my children shall know of his love and strength through me.
— Marisol

Two reading assignments explore the important role our ancestors play in our characters and our lifestyles:

    1) "Notes of a Native Son," by James Baldwin
    2) "In Search of Our Mothers' Gardens," by Alice
       Walker (see Note below).

To encourage active reading, students write journal reflections on what they read. These reading logs can be as simple as "What do you notice?" "What do you like?" "What do you wonder?"

The next sequence of exercises continues the thinking about family history. Students create their own family crests, using words, images, and color to represent their ethnic or national origins, their traditions, religions, and family occupations. In addition, I ask students to write a family motto that would represent a family value, belief, or tradition. Again, I share my own drawing with them first, explaining why I have chosen these words and images to represent my family. While I give them an outline of a traditional crest as a guide (see Appendix A, p. 59), I encourage them to change, enlarge, or recreate it to suit their own concept of their family history. Andrew, for example, rejected the conventional crest shape and drew an outline of Africa to shape his crest and express his origins. Others made similar modifications. (See Figure 2 on the next page.) Students share their completed crest with the class, explaining the meaning and significance of the words and images they have chosen to

NOTE: Sources for all assignments in this and following chapters are listed in Appendix B, p. 61.

Figure 2

symbolize their family. This activity is followed by a short reflection on their heritage.

The students' next writing assignment draws on the factual material of the family tree, the tribute to an ancestor, and the creative and symbolic material of the family crest. The poem "Heritage" by Linda Hogan (see

Appendix B), in which the author describes the different qualities she has inherited from her family, is an excellent lead-in to this assignment. The readings and in-class activities are incorporated into a definition or description of their own heritage:

> Describe your character in terms of heredity, deducing from what you know of your forebears; or tell what characteristic habit or feature of your personality seems to have come most directly from your ethnic, national, or familial origins (adapted from *New Worlds of Literature*, p. 325).

Again, these are quick writes, done in class, which help to generate an abundance of material for use in later, formal assignments.

> *I do not consider myself as an American, but as an Asian-American. Almost all of my values and customs are a mixture of both cultures. A perfect example of this would be my name; even though I have changed it to an American name, Jamie, I also keep My Le, the Chinese name that was given to me by my parents.* — My Le

The next example is from another of my students; she is adopted:

> *I was born half Native American and half Danish. I did not choose my parents: I did not choose my background: they were given to me Unfortunately, nobody gets to choose what their heritage will be. But then I guess that's the fun of it. I know what my heritage is and I am proud of it. It is what makes me an individual, different from everyone else. Everyone should be proud of their heritage and learn about it as much as they can, because heritage is what makes each of us special individuals. However, that which allows an individual to find identity, also causes many conflicts between people who find differences amongst each other.* — Kirsten

Clearly, thinking about their family history is relevant to adopted students whether they know anything about their biological parents or not.

> *As I wrote earlier, the subject of heritage is a hard one for me. I don't know if I do things like my natural mom or dad. I will never know if I look like my biological grandparents; my habits and jestures start with me as I see it. However, I can say that some of my habits and jestures come from my adoptive family. Some people even say that my mom and I look alike. We have a very deep family life that dwells on our grandparents. We do a lot of things with my mother's parents; as a result, I know a lot about their lives and even their parents. I consider their lives and their parents lives to be my heritage, but always wonder about my biological heritage. Where do I really come from? What do my parents look like? Will I die of heart disease when I am forty-five? ... These things will always be in the back of my mind, especially when I decide to have a family of my own.* — Andrew

While the writing here is personal and informal, it also requires some analysis of why and how students have become who they are, how their family histories may have affected their character, and how they view themselves.

ESSAY #1 The students' first formal essay assignment is "Looking Back," growing out of "Noting Down" (to use Moffett's term):

> Describe/define your heritage and its importance to your character, lifestyle, and/or beliefs.

Students use a combination of rhetorical modes in developing their essays, including description, narration, definition, and analysis. Using the plenitude of writing generated by activities and readings, students "mine" their notebooks for ideas and examples to develop their definitions of heritage. Students are required to write several drafts of their essays. The second draft is read aloud in writing groups that have formed early in the course. There they have worked with reading logs and journal freewrites, as well as drafts of essay assignments. For response to the second draft of Essay #1, group members are asked to write answers to the following questions about the draft they hear:

1. What is the most memorable part of this essay?
2. What is this draft's greatest strength?
3. Does the essay address all parts of the assignment?
4. Was any part of the essay particularly confusing?
5. Ask at least one question about the material presented in the essay.

The author of the piece is asked to respond to questions about his or her own paper:

1. What do you like best about this essay?
2. Of what are you least sure?
3. What do you see as your most important point?
4. What is your support for that point?
5. What do you want to get from your group? Be specific. Get it!
6. After discussing your paper with your group, answer the following: How can you improve this paper? What are your plans for revision?

The groups then discuss their responses, beginning with the writer's answer to question #5. Students revise their papers for the next class, at which I give a mini-lesson on a needed skill — paragraph development, coherence, focus, punctuation, and so on. They revise, edit, and polish their papers, turning in typed drafts to me for my response. My comments focus, as a rule, on content and on those skills students are now acquiring. This is sometimes followed by a conference. I do not grade individual essays since each assignment may be revised as often as necessary throughout the course. I grade only the entire notebook at the end of the class, so students can continue to refine their ideas and their writing skills.

In the following excerpts from polished student essays, it is clear that defining the most important point requires students to think critically.

> *People seldom ask me what my ethnicity is because just by looking at my black hair and dark skin people can usually tell. I consider myself to be Mexican-American, meaning that I am an American as a result of being born in the United States, yet I am also of a Mexican descent which I take into account as a major influence in my life. My heritage consists of all the Mexican customs, traditions, myths, and Catholic religion, as well as speaking the Spanish language. These have been characteristics which have made me who I am today.*

> *All cultures have their negative as well as positive traditions, for the value is not necessarily to preserve the whole culture, but much rather the good that the culture provides for its people. For instance, in the Mexican culture, a negative characteristic which has played a part in women being seen as inferior is what is known as 'machismo.' Machismo is the glorification or acknowledgment of power given to males. Latin males are viewed as strong and aggressive; whereas, the Latin woman is seen as submissive and weak. Should this tradition of the powerful male continue as a part of our culture?*

Rosa goes on to give examples from her childhood of the way chores were divided between herself and her brothers, and the specific gender roles enforced in her family. In addition, she gives further examples of social and religious gender roles. She advocates a rejection of the limitations placed on women by her culture.

> *One can see that by following all these customs and traditions, just to preserve the culture, generation after generation has been kept back from progressing to their fullest capabilities.*

> *Educating myself has helped me to view how chicana women are stereotyped even amongst their own family, not to mention our society. Through education I have been able to remove myself one step from this cultural cycle and examine it objectively.* — Rosa

Clearly, what begins as a narrative description becomes analytical and speculative. The movement from looking inward to looking outward, from the personal to the universal, occurs quite naturally in the course of the writing assignment. Already the bridge between personal and transpersonal writing has begun to be built. Defining an abstract term like "heritage" requires students to think critically, to take their personal experience and use it as a foundation on which to build later discussions about culture and its value.

Here are excerpts from Diem's essay, "Spring Flower," and a reflection by her about the writing of it.

Spring Flower

My name, Diem-Trang, is the Vietnamese flower blooming a warm tone in Spring. This plant grows from the raw earth of my homeland, its vibrant red petals and green leaves enriched with sunlight, its roots drawing strength from within the mineral laden soil. As the winds sweep across the mountains, the tall grass whispers as the wind brushes it, while the flower's tender stalk, too, is shaped by nature's forces.

I am this young plant, influenced by the whisper of generations reflected through the character of my mother and father, struggling to draw on their experience ... being shaped by their wisdom. But the tides of war, a juggernaut of human nature, tears the dark soil apart, unsettling the roots of plants. Like all disasters of nature, mother earth can regenerate and replenish. For trees and plants can be grown anew and replanted ... I am like a replanted seedling, adjusting to new American soil. I am a plant strengthened by the winds of past ancestors and by the experiences drawn from a foreign land.

However strongly my roots grip to the new soil, the memories and color of my past are remembered through my father's tales of the vibrant land of his youth. These revisits to the soil of my ancestors reminds me who I am and the significance of my past. Indeed, it was my father who came up with the name Diem-Trang ... he who grew up in a small rural village a hundred miles from Hanoi, spoiled rotten, being the only son. Dad grew up knowing what communism proffered: starvation and oppression. Perhaps seeing villagers wrap banana leaves over clothing to evade the cold only to catch sickness from the penetrating chill seeping through the leaves is what made him so ardently opposed to communism in the North.

In my dad, I see his love for the free past ... his vision of unscathed Vietnam: a land covered thick with trees, a serene land of green rice paddies. Through his tales, I see in vivid colors the kind expressions of laboring farmers tending rice seedlings, wearing cone shaped straw hats to escape the sun's pervading beams. His memories of the past are portraits of the fields, mountains, and endless beaches. Once, he vehemently claimed that the North, where he was born, was more beautiful (except for the stigma of communism, of course) than all other parts of the country, arguing that the spectacular white sanded beaches complement the raw beauty of the green landscape.

Through such descriptions, I can see the physical landscape of my heritage where my roots were first entrenched. It was a land dominated by the innocence of nature. There is never a time when I tire of hearing his tales of the land and all that it contained. There used to be a stream which flowed near my father's village. In the scorching heat of the summer season, he would go fishing, catching big fresh-water fish swimming through the clear waters which rippled over the pebbled ground. Through his words, I appreciate the land where my roots drew strength and a rich culture. I am reminded of images like the fresh water stream flowing by his village, the green rice paddies, and kind people through his tales. His stories are colors of my natal land.

However, I am the young plant that was enriched not only by the tales of my father's youth and of the land where I first greeted sunlight and ushered forth life, but also by the other wind that blew: my mother's stolid character introduced me to the meaning of persistence, pride, and survival. As she nurtured me, watering me with her advice so that I could understand and thrive like a flower budding in fertile soil, my stem drew in the family values which she instilled in me.

These values that I admire in my mother are traits which define her character and my heritage. She was a born survivor. Being the younger of a set of twins, brought to life frail and feeble, she was sent to the North to be cared for by her grandmother while her twin sister remained in warm South Vietnam. Mom says that her mother separated them so that both of them could thrive. But it was my mother who survived in the coldest of winter, and who learned to obey and work hard at all orders of her strict grandmother.

It was this same instinct for survival that compelled her to fight for her way of life in Vietnam, even with communist rule. And it was the same instinct which made her sell her fabric business and her house to flee. What she carried on her back when we fled the town of Long Xuyen on an early dawn in 1979 were not material possessions, but life and hope. I was on my mother's back that crack of the morning, gleefully watching the turbid waters swirl past Mom's knees as we made way to the boat in the distance which would bring the family to the Malaysian refugee camp. With Mother's persistence, we were able to survive through the Malaysian refugee camp. Even with the little rationed food that local officials distributed,

15

Mother made do and we never went hungry. In America, when everyone else who had fled in 1975 seemed to have so much and we so little, it was again her dutiful persistence and optimism that helped us not to notice ...

I can still remember the boat trip across the South China Sea when the ocean waves creeped up to the sides of the boat precariously. People crowded below deck used pieces of soap to stuff the tiny leaks of the boat. I, like others, awaited the outcome of the forceful night storm which rocked the wooden boat, making too many sea sick. But nature has its calmer moments, and the storm subsided. After several days at sea, due to a miracle and the skill of the captain, a dark fisherman from Long Xuyen, we made it to Malaysian shore. To this day I still recall the crystal waters and colorful tropical fish which swam as I carefully waded to a shore dotted with towering palms and sea gulls gliding midair above. The beautiful picture I remember is of bedraggled and feeble people crying for joy as they sank their feet to the white sanded shore in a triumph.

The celebration and sense of victory soon subsided as we adjusted to the refugee camp, however. There, we lived in a shelter with no walls and cooked in a pit hollowed out from the dirt. Money was soon forgotten by my parents because we didn't have any. I remember when one of our neighbors, who somehow got a hold of a bunch of fresh grapes, offered me two. Eagerly, I thanked her and tasted the juicy sweet and sour grape delightfully. The last grape I had to save for Hieu, my brother, and I gave it to my mom to keep where I couldn't reach it. But unfortunately, my eyes could travel to higher heights. For a very long time, I started at the green grape, eyeing its round, plump shape. For a very long time, I was a hungry child, wanting the taste of fresh fruit a second time. I sat there dreamily, until my eldest brother snatched the grape and gave it to me.

In America, I can have a lot more than two grapes. In America, we do not have to fight back our hunger. There is an entire bag of grapes in the refrigerator that my parents bought fresh at the farmer's market last weekend. They don't seem like such a big deal to me now ...

Wishing to have a full stomach, or for another taste of fresh fruit is what makes me value the life I have at the present. I am proud of the fact that our constitution protects citizens from a totalitarian state and guarantees freedom for all. I understand now how precious freedom is for my family and I risked our lives and left our homeland for this commodity. I am shaped by fleeing my country razed by the fire of war and defeat. My refugee experience is the part of me that struggled for under-standing, it is the bridge between two distinct ways of life formed by the forces of war and circumstance.

Hence, I am the seedling replanted and shaped by the forces of war and by the character and experiences drawn from the wisdom of my parents. In American soil, I continue to be influenced by the voice of my ancestors whispering in the wind. For in this rich earth, I am still the Vietnamese flower blooming in Spring. When the petals open to face the world, it is strong, the roots gripped to memories of its native soil and enriched through new experiences drawn to the stem from its new environment.

Journal

I enjoyed writing this piece and was happy to see my original fragmented stories connected through the image of the flower. Your suggestion of carrying through with this image really helped with the transitions. I think writing this piece helped me to find my perspective on my personal experiences as a refugee. To me, writing the paper made sense ... it seemed to fit in to my life and so I felt comfortable piecing the previous stories together under the theme of my heritage.

PHASE II: Heritage as History

The next sequence of reading, thinking, and writing assignments moves students into the area of "Looking Into." By looking into an aspect of history, students make the personal academic and the academic personal. First students read "In Search of History" by Barbara Tuchman (see Appendix C, page 67), a short piece about her writing process, sources and methods for research, and about the purpose of writing history, which she explains should be to recapture imaginatively the way it was while at the same time staying within the evidence:

> *Through this forest of special pleading the historian gropes his way, trying to recapture the truth of past events and find out 'what really happened.' He discovers that truth is subjective and separate, made up of little bits seen through a kaleidoscope; when the cylinder is shaken the countless colored fragments form a new picture. Yet they are the same fragments that made a different picture a moment earlier. This is the problem inherent in the records left by actors in past events. (p. 401)*

Students also read the poem "Ellis Island" by Joseph Bruchac, which describes the immigration of families into America through the famous landmark in New York City.

After a discussion of the Tuchman piece and a tour of the library, students choose and complete one of two research topics:

> The coming to America of your family or ethnic group OR an historical event one or more of your ancestors did or could have participated in.

At UCSB I was able to obtain the help of a research librarian to whom I gave a copy of my students' assignment, so she was able to tailor a tour and lecture to their specific task and needs. Using herself as an example, she took my students along the research trail she had followed, describing the reference materials and showing them where to find them in the library (Appendix C). My students found this to be one of the most valuable experiences of the term.

ESSAY #2 With their completed project and their research materials, notes, and bibliography, students are ready to write their second essay. As with the research project assignment, they have two options (as a rule Native American students choose the second option):

> 1. Having found basic factual information about the coming to America of your own national, or ethnic, or tribal group, use your research to write a documented essay that traces the circumstances and events which may have affected their coming and their life once they arrived. You may use family stories to develop this discussion or your "speculative" imagination to fill in the details of what it must have been like for them (This is adapted from the research paper assignment on page 461 in *New Worlds of Literature.)*

> 2. Having identified and researched an historical event in which one or more of your ancestors did or could have participated, use the facts you have gathered in your research to write a documented

essay which describes how this event may have affected your forbears. If you know a family story about this ancestor you may use it in conjunction with historical research material. If you are only speculating about his or her involvement, use your "speculative" imagination as well as historical fact to place him or her in the context of the event.

In either case what you are attempting to do is (as suggested by Barbara Tuchman) create a narrative history — not a story, but a telling of an historical event from a subjective point of view, "to recapture the truth of past events and find out 'what really happened.'"

Again students write several drafts of this essay assignment; the first is a quick draft in class. Students put away all notes and books, and using only a brief outline, write everything they know now about their topic in fifty minutes. This difficult, even painful, process helps students to clarify what they know and also forces them to put their knowledge into their own words, thereby avoiding the turgid prose of research notes. The next draft is read to their writing group, using the following questions to elicit responses:

1. Does the title peak your interest? Is it inventive and original?
2. Does the introduction draw you in, make you want to know more? By the end of the first paragraph are you sure what the essay's main point/thesis is? In one or two sentences restate the main point.
3. Does the writer give enough concrete and specific examples to illustrate and prove his or her points? Which example stands out in your mind?
4. Were you always sure why information was being given you? Were you confused at any

21

point? Which part did you have the most trouble understanding?

5. Is the conclusion satisfying? Did it seem to tie up the essay without restating or summarizing the main points? Did it reach out to make personal or universal observations about the implications of the theme? Describe your feeling when you heard the conclusion; use a simile if you can — "I felt like… " "The conclusion is like…"

6. Are the quotations cited and punctuated correctly within the text? Are they gracefully integrated? Are the Works Cited and Works Consulted pages correctly prepared?

The author of the draft responds to the following questions:

1. Does your introduction clearly and specifically state the issue you will cover in your essay? (It isn't enough to say that you will discuss "your family's part in the Mexican Revolution." You need to let readers know your strategy for exploring the issue, and give a hint about the conclusions you will draw.)
   a) Underline your essay's main point.
   b) What can you do to make your introduction more inviting?

2. Does each paragraph clearly state what it will address, and does it address only one idea at a time? Does it progress in levels of generality from the general to the very specific? Do your specific examples support and illustrate your claims? Does each paragraph connect back to your main idea? Does each shift in thought contain a smooth transition from the previous paragraph to the next?

a) Underline the topic sentence (or articulate in the margins the main idea) for each paragraph in the body of your essay.

b) Make notes on paragraphs that need a clear statement of their main idea. Check the levels of generality — do you give enough concrete and specific examples? What details can you add?

3. Are you pushing throughout your essay for the deepest implications of your topic, putting your specific illustrations to work for you in making more universally relevant observations? I cannot say this too many times: keep asking yourself, "SO WHAT?"

4. Does your conclusion do more than summarize your essay? Have you tried to venture an opinion on what the personal and/or universal implications might be of this topic? Can you finish with an anecdote that illustrates the main point of your essay? Does your conclusion tie in with your introduction?

After another revision of the paper, students exchange papers for final editing. The polished and typed draft is turned in for my response. As I read these papers, I am looking for a balanced presentation of personal story with research material. Of course, in addition to other writing skills such as focus, organization, coherence, and development, students are demonstrating their ability to integrate documentation gracefully into their texts as well as to punctuate quotations correctly and prepare a properly formatted Works Cited page.

The research paper or documented essay takes students another step toward transpersonal writing while still retaining their personal investment in the topic. The following are excerpts from student essays representing both options. In her essay entitled "In Search of a Better Life," Rosa vividly describes the reasons for her family coming to the United States from Mexico.

> *In a village lived my uncle Juan who has a shack which only consisted of two rooms. In the small room slept the whole family; at night it was so stuffy that the children could barely breathe. The other room was everything else including the kitchen as well as the living room. There was no plumbing and therefore they had to go far to get water or seek for a hidden place to use the restroom. As a result of the Mexican tradition in which the male must be the head of the household, Juan was made responsible to put the bread on the table and provide the basic necessities to his family. He was forced to work long hours and has to accept the miserable wage he was paid even though his daily life earnings were insufficient to provide his household with adequate living conditions.*

Having described the family situation which prompted emigration, Rosa goes on to explain the economic conditions in Mexico which caused so many families to leave between 1940 and 1960. But she also explains the situation they encountered once they reached the United States. She uses her historical research to make general her family's specific experience.

Veronica begins her essay, "Talking About a Chicano," with a description of how her brother and sister entered the U. S.:

> *It was a rainy day around mid April when, for the first time, my brother and sister visit the United States. They carried with them a carton box with all their belongings and covered it with a plastic bag for when they had to swim across the river, their belongings wouldn't get wet. After they were in the United States and were able to take off their muddy 'huaraches' and soaked clothes, and after a good night sleep they had lots of time to forget all the insults of the border patrol and the pain and suffering.*

Her essay is based on research into what happens to Mexican emigrants once they have successfully arrived in the U.S. She also tells stories of friends and relatives to describe the reception and the living conditions of Mexican emigrants, and the resulting negative effects on their self-esteem:

> *Unfortunately, the person may not feel worthy of being treated well. Some go to the extreme of denying part of who they are. For Mexican/Chicanos this is a real dilemma that may be the reason for not having one set level. Some deny their back-ground others prefer to be considered more American than Mexican or vice versa. Import is given to lighter skin because it's related to the dominant culture and darker skin is rejected.*

Although Veronica has not made herself perfectly clear here, this confusion is a manifestation of the thinking going on — she is trying to explain something she has seen and read about. Rather than just reporting, she is analyzing.

My Le describes her journey to the United States from Viet Nam:

> *The little boat was crowded and there was not enough food or water for all the people on the boat. Fortunately, we reached Indonesia in only five days without being stopped by pirates. When we arrived on a small island in Indonesia, we did not have a place to live. We had to build our own house with palm tree trunks for foundations and roof and walls. There was no running water, and we had to dig holes in the ground to use as bathrooms.*

In her essay entitled "Vivir con Miedo (Living with Fear)," Marisol describes the arrest of her great-grandfather as a revolutionary by the Federales during the Mexican Revolution. She combines historical research with a family story, placing her great-grandfather's experience within the larger context of the historical event. She describes the causes and goals of the revolution, provides important names and dates, but what enlivens her account is her family story, enriching the reader's under-standing and transforming the cold historical facts.

As the sun shines brightly on one of the beautiful green valleys of Mexico, a young boy stands terrified in front of a small firing squad. The beauty of the warm summer day greatly contrasts with the fear of the young boy and the hatred of the Federales (the Mexican army). The crime the young prisoner is accused of is resembling a revolutionary ... With their weapons aimed and ready, the Federales await with anticipation for the word which will enable them to end the life of their young prisoner.

The air is filled with hate and fear; the tension is thick and almost all consuming. Suddenly the thundering hooves of a horse are heard and for a split second the tension is broken ... the rider is a friend of the soldiers and of the young captive ... the captain orders his soldiers to lower their weapons and to let the young man go free. There is disappointment on the faces of the men, but they obey their superior ... the young man is relieved ... for the moment he is safe, until he is again mistaken for a rebel or an 'hacendado' (one who sympathizes with the Federales) and perhaps the next time his life will not be spared.

Through her great-grandfather's experience Marisol dramatically portrays the confusing reality of war, as she concludes:

My great-grandfather was not a soldier for either side, yet because he lived in a war zone, he was constantly in danger of being confused as the 'Enemy.' He feared both groups, those who fought to keep him in a sort of slavery (the Federales) and those who were supposedly fighting to give him land and freedom.

Through their research, students find themselves to be a part of history. They come to value their stories as important elements in that history. In addition, they learn library and research skills, how to write from sources while at the same time using their own ideas, and how to integrate quotations into their essays. They also move from firsthand to secondhand information, and as Moffett says, "that's part of the movement from personal writing to essay writing" (p. 5).

PHASE III: Examining Values and Traditions

In order to set up the "Thinking Through" stage of the sequence, students focus on a specific problem. The conflict between family values and traditions of the family and those of society — including the university — is an issue students are often forced to confront. Through a series of activities, discussions, and writings, students identify their cultural and personal values, as well as those offered outside the traditions of their cultural community.

First, we have a class "show and tell." Students bring an artifact that represents some aspect of their cultural identity (music, food, art, clothing) and talk about its significance to their family or culture. For example, some students bring family cooking pots, hats, jewelry; some tell folk tales, play music, or describe holiday or religious traditions or rituals. Diem brought her mother's traditional Vietnamese dress. In her journal she wrote,

> *I feel it reflects Vietnamese culture. The 'auo gio' is my mother's — the navy material covered with the hand embroidered cranes and gray curls. The styling is very simple and conservative, matching the Vietnamese simple, yet unique culture. These long dresses were a sign of prosperity — women would wear them before communism took over, a sign of happiness like on 'tet,' the Vietnamese New Year.*

Sal performed a traditional Basque sheep call. Homer cooked "lumpia," a traditional Filipino dish, to share with the class. Leslie brought a handmade lace pillowcase made by her grandmother, and Sarah showed us a quilt that has been in her family for many years. Adriana shared her great-grandmother's wedding ring, a precious symbol of the first woman in her family to be married out of slavery. Elisa showed us a picture of her mother wearing wooden shoes and told us about her family's Christmas ritual of placing the shoes on the window sill to be filled with treats by Saint Nicholas. Through religious articles, old photographs, jewelry, and story telling, students were not only able to take pride in their heritage by talking about it with their peers, but to see what kinds of things those with different backgrounds value.

The next journal writings on this topic are a series of five to ten minute responses to four songs concerned with problems that can come with honoring the values and traditions of one's cultural community. These journal entries will help to form the basis for later class discussion as well as prewriting for the next essay assignment. This "discovery" writing plays a crucial role in the unfolding sequence of assignments. I play a song and then ask students to freewrite for about ten minutes in response to a question or prompt.

"Tradition" *(Fiddler on the Roof)*: What role does gender play in the expectations of your family members? Are there any expectations you wish to depart from? Can you? Do you?

In my family there has been a tradition of men play/work, women housework/kids with different roles that each kid should take depending on your gender. The roles are not very just, for if you are a woman you would end up having the worst, tuffest, and less appreciated part, the house. If you are a female at a young age you would be given responsibility of doing the chores around the house ... I would like to break away from this custom. — Veronica

"Jet Song" *(Westside Story)*: How does it feel to belong to a "tribe"? What are the pros and cons of membership?

... it is something more than just skin color or country it is everything that has sorrounded you since your were small. I belong to the Chicano or Mexican tribe (group) ... we want to still belong to that group of people we left behind when my mother decided to come over and cross the river as a mojada 'wetback.' There is a conflict here though because the group that we actually were part of when all my family was down here was of la 'Raza' low-income barrio kind of people that could get along fine without speaking English, for in the factories all the 'mayordomos' (supervisors) are Mexican-Americans. 'La Raza' stands for the people that share the same economic, political and basicly same ideology ... a group of people which stand together in unity. But most of the times this is not so ... Whenever someone does get out and betters himself, we no longer share the same economic, political and ideology a resentment starts to grow and he/she is not longer considered one of us. Unfortunately, he is not considered one of them either. Too good to be Mexican, not enough to be American. Sad but true.

'Go back where you came from.' I've heard this in many songs ... That we are too many already they try to discourage migrants from the small town not to go into the city or capital or to the 'other side.' ... They say that at least back there they have their beans and families and down here you struggle and have to spend days without the love or the peace of your hearts. That you live in constant fear that the 'Migra' immigration will deport you back to the border. After you have taken jobs at half price minimum wage to send money back home and keep the kids fed ... after you take jobs that a 'gringo' would not take and work the hours he would not handle you are told you are taking their jobs away from them

... they are here because they have the 'American Dream' to be economicly free ... — Veronica

"A Boy Like That" *(Westside Story)*: Does your "tribe" have any restrictions about marrying outside it?

Maybe it has to do with that all my boyfriends have been latinos. I wonder what reaction they'll have if I started dating a Philipino or a black man. I think my mom would not oppose ... for she would never want to limit me in my life. Maybe because it's hard to actually get someone from another cultural background interested in you or you interested in them. I don't know it's kind of funny how without knowing it but you stick to people you have things in common with, well, in some cases, it might only be skin color.

"America" *(Westside Story)*: What are the benefits of adapting to or adopting a new culture? What are the drawbacks to giving up your heritage wholly or in part? What are the difficulties in doing so if you wish?

Adapting to America has strengthened me as a person be-cause I've had the benefit of two cultures to draw experiences on. From American society I've learned about independence and believing in myself. For in America, I can be whatever I want in life ... However, the drawback is blending too fully in this rich land. I must realize that I am still Vietnamese and must adhere to my culture. In my opinion, I think I do, but keeping up with my language is difficult (since I left my country at an early age). There is always the dread of being labeled 'Americanized,' the term for abandoning your cul-ture. However, adapting to America as a Vietnamese, I realized that full integration in this new society is not feasible not only in the respect that I wish to retain my culture, but also

in the regards that I am Vietnamese in a land dominated by
Caucasians — white culture. — Diem

Other songs could be used for this exercise — Bruce Springstein's "Born in the USA," Neil Diamond's "They Come to America," *South Pacific's* "You have to be Carefully Taught."

In addition to the songs, I assign several readings in fiction and non-fiction which also explore the issue of conflicting cultural values and traditions, and how people caught between two cultures cope.

1. "Everyday Use" by Alice Walker
2. "Obachan" by Gail Y. Miyaksaki
3. "No Name Woman" by Maxine Hong Kingston
4. "Migrants: Transients or Settlers?" by Elena Padilla
5. "Indians Today and Their Fight for Survival" in *The Indian Heritage of America* by Alvin M. Josephy, Jr.

The first part of Phase III, the values and traditions section of the writing sequence, deals generally with the personal issue of cultural identity. The next part of this third phase deals more specifically with an important aspect of heritage: language. Two valuable readings are "Aria: A Memoir of a Bilingual Childhood" by Richard Rodriguez and "If Black English Isn't a Language, Then Tell Me, What Is?" by James Baldwin. For students for whom English is a second language or for students who speak a dialect of English, these readings speak to some important issues: the value of English, the loss of a native or primary language as a result of assimilation, the social bias against non-standard dialects. For students who are native speakers of standard English, the readings as well as the responses by the other students challenge their unexamined assumptions about language. Students write two journal entries which encourage them to engage actively with the texts and which provide material for subsequent group discussions and debate.

Discuss language as a "political instrument, means, and proof of power."

Discuss language as a key to identity (personal and social) *(Modern American Prose,* "Suggestions for Writing," p. 41).

After exploring their own values and traditions, hearing about the experiences of others in the class, and reading different treatments of the issues involved, students can move on to a "Thinking Through" activity: the Argument Clinic. In this activity students practice the methods of argumentation, including taking a stand and supporting it with reasons, explanations, and evidence, as well as challenging the stand and supporting evidence of the other side, and then defending and refining their own argument. The class is offered two propositions:

Young people should cherish the values and traditions of their cultural backgrounds.

Young people should be free to ignore old values and traditions in building a new society (*New Worlds of Literature*, suggested "Argumentative Papers," p. 325).

I prepare students for the Argument Clinic by defining argument as a rhetorical mode and by demonstrating models of argumentative development on the board. First, students freewrite for five minutes on each proposition. Then the class is divided into two groups and each group is assigned one of the propositions. Each group discusses the case to be made for its proposition, finds examples and/or evidence from the readings and from members' own experiences to support the case. They develop an outline with the proposition as their thesis, providing supporting statements/reasons, and examples/evidence. Each group writes an outline on the board. Each side presents its case, using the outline on the board; then the other group has an opportunity to challenge and to question the case. The presenting group may then respond by revising the outline with qualifying statements and/or additional proofs or expanded explanations of the statements. Following the presentation and discussion of the two propositions, students freewrite again on whether or not their opinion has been changed or expanded by the discussion. At this point most students are inclined to accept both propositions as true and valuable with qualifications of one kind or another.

ESSAY #3 In this assignment, students have the option of writing an argument that supports one of the propositions or of writing a discussion in which they can discuss the value of both propositions and how they personally reconcile the conflict between the two in their own minds and lives. As with the two previous essays, students write multiple drafts, share their drafts with their writing group, and receive constructive responses. In addition, however, when their polished and typed draft is prepared and ready to turn in to me, I ask them to adopt my role and read their own papers, evaluating and responding as objectively as possible. This exercise in self assessment is remarkably successful; as a rule, I merely have to agree with their remarks and expand on them. Following are excerpts from one student essay:

> *Every society changes over time to accommodate the wants and needs of the people living in it. Many different types of changes can occur; economic, racial, cultural, pollution density ... The question is while all these changes are occurring should people cherish the values and traditions they inherited from their ancestors or should they be free to ignore them? There are more than a few ways to argue this issue. Some may say that old traditions can't just be trashed because they are tightly woven into the backbone of society's everyday life. They shape and give order to society, and identity and self-possession to the individual. Others will argue that in order to change the society the first step has to be in changing the most basic part of the society, which are the values and traditions. I think in order to provide a balanced decision both choices should be taken into consideration. There can be no absolute, but there are pros and cons to both sides of the*

argument, these will have a heavy effect on the outcome of the changed society.— Kirsten

My Le cites the story by Maxine Hong Kingston, "No Name Woman," as an example of how traditions that are morally wrong should be ignored or challenged. Reba maintains that "the past is the foundation for the present and the future and without it, we would have no sense of identity. The past supports the future like the foundation of a building; the new builds upon the old. Whether or not we reject or accept the old values and traditions, they do act as factors in who we are and what we believe; therefore, they cannot be ignored."

Clearly, these students have crossed Moffett's bridge from personal to transpersonal writing. They are able to take ideas from the texts they have read and discussed to support their own positions; they have learned to think through an issue, draw their own conclusions, and write essays in which they coherently express themselves. The intellectual rigor of this sequence of assignments expands the students' cognitive powers and prepares them to think through and write about difficult problems when they are asked to do so in other academic courses.

PHASE IV: Social Issues

The first reading in this section of the heritage sequence is the personal narrative by Gary Soto, "Like Mexicans," in which he describes his decision to marry a Japanese woman in spite of his own fears and his family's objections. The issue of "mixed marriages" is one we've encountered before in our reading (see "Obachan" and "My Mother's Stories"). In class, we discuss what Soto means by saying that his girl friend's Japanese family are "just like Mexicans." Diem wrote in her journal:

> *I liked this piece because it made me feel that through all the tensions over race and a predominate white culture, there is a sector who live their lives free from such racial boundaries as in the case of the Mexican man and the Japanese woman he chose to marry. I wonder what the speaker's future life is like — how does he and his family fit into society? Do their children have difficulties finding their cultural identity amid two such distinctive ways of life: Japanese and Mexican?*

In this story an important social dilemma is resolved happily; however, the student foresees conflict nevertheless. And the next several reading assignments, in fact, pose similar questions about cultural conflict which are not easily answered. Students take turns reading the poems aloud; then they write journal entries, defining the issue or problem presented by each piece. Each short freewriting is followed by voluntary sharing and discussion of the poem and its central issue — stereotyping, racial tokenism, living between two cultures, racism, the gap of understanding between cultures, the desirability of ethnic studies. Several students' brief journal responses to five of the pieces follow.

"The Bridge Poem" by Donna Kate Rushin
> *The issue here is other people trying to use her to prove their humanness — the speaker is sick of being mediator for prejudiced people trying to prove they are not.* — Diem

"In Response to Executive Order 9066: ALL AMERICANS OF JAPANESE DESCENT MUST REPORT TO RELOCATION CENTERS" by Dwight Okita
> *The issue is of being alienated and discriminated by a white society even though one is [American] on the inside.* — Diem

"Song of the Breed" by Gogisgi
> *This poem describes the confusion of being mixed with two races.* — Erin

"So Mexicans Are Taking Jobs from Americans" by Jimmy Santiago Baca
> *The focus of this piece expresses the white society using the Mexicans as scapegoats for their economic woes.* — Diem

> *The ignorance of the white man who is stuck in poverty ... causes a tension between them and other races. They blame the Mexicans for taking their jobs, but the Mexicans are still poor, they're just trying to survive.* — Erin

"I'm Sitting in My History Class" by Richard Olivas
> *It's ignorance toward the [society's] diversity.* — Elisa

Having the students write first before attempting a discussion insures that each student has something to say. Other poems to read and discuss in class include: "Sure You Can Ask Me A Personal Question" by Diane Burns and "Sonrisas" by Pat Mora.

The class then breaks up into small groups, each taking a poem to look at closely. Each group presents their findings to the class, leads a discussion, and assigns another journal writing, offering a prompt or question based on their presentation. For example, the group analyzing "The Bridge" offered this writing prompt for the class: How's the author made to feel a token in our society?

> *She is considered an object, 1) because she is a woman and 2) she is black. She seems to have to put up with the endless chain of questions of 'How does it feel?' and 'What's it like?' then at the same time ignoramuses use her to justify their own prejudices and that is what she is sick of.* — Iris

About the poem "So Mexicans Are Taking Jobs From Americans," students were asked: Compare and contrast the values of America with those supported in the poem.

> *White farmers are selling out to big businessmen. Only a few people own everything, while the rest of us work for them and are only able to buy necessities from it. We aren't giving the children a chance to live because poverty cannot be overcome.* — Erin

These readings, freewritings, and class discussions prepare the students to find their own focus for their fourth essay assignment.

ESSAY #4 After these readings, discussions, and freewritings, students are assigned a "position paper" in which they will focus on one issue or problem, describe it, analyze it and speculate on possible solutions.

> We've spent the last nine weeks thinking, reading, writing, and talking about heritage. Now it is time for you to reflect on our exploration of this topic and decide what you think about it at this point. You will

need to find your own focus for this paper, ask your own question. What is your position on heritage? What is the most important point you want to make about heritage in general or your own heritage in particular? Consider the following questions: Whose ideas do you agree with, whose do you reject? Is the study of heritage divisive or community build-ing? How does/should/can a multicultural society address the diversity of its population? Mine your writer's notebook for material. Reread your journal entries, your research material. As in all the writing you have done this quarter, thoughtful analysis with examples is important.

The following excerpts demonstrate clearly the kind of thoughtful analysis the students are now able to do without much direct interference on my part.

In her essay "Political Split: Unproductive Separatism," Iris explains her abrupt indoctrination into ethnic labels when she arrived at the university and identified herself as Mexican " … I hadn't understood any reason for the existence of such technical terms as 'Chicano/a' or the sensitivity toward 'Hispanic,' of the significance of identifying myself as 'Mexican-American'." Later she declares that at the university ethnic studies "have apparently not emphasized the importance of understand-ing other cultures."

Colleen writes about the stereotypes of Asian-Americans as a "Model Minority":

> *It is ironic how the image of the Asian-American has changed in the recent past. The image portrayed of the typical Asian has shifted from an uncivilized foreigner to a model minority. Perhaps it is the intense turnabout of overcoming racism that the Asian culture made that attracts so much attention to their phenomenal success. Asian Americans have validated their progress and by reasons, not of their own, socially formed the image of the model minority. The constant pressure to be*

above average has put a strain on the students that has not weakened, but in fact, has strengthened in the past years and increased media attention.

The desire to keep up with the Asian image is not easy. I constantly feel obligated to always excel in studies, primarily because of the pressure society places on me. I am only half Asian, but society views me as Asian and therefore I must be academically wise. I do not want to have to work up to somebody else's expectations, I want to be the best I can be for myself not for someone else.

Using the Jimmy Santiago Baca poem we read in foundation, Shane wrote his essay "Is It Really Their Fault?" about the idea that Mexicans steal jobs from Americans.

The Mexicans aren't physically stealing occupations from Americans. They don't arrive to some field or factory with baseball bats or guns threatening to hurt or kill if they aren't allowed to work. Rather Mexicans simply search for any job that will feed the family. Sure everyone would like a little extra money, but it is very rare to see Hispanics from Mexico immigrate, become an instant millionaire and fit into the American Way ... Major factors that support this ideal are, most Hispanics are raised with strong religious beliefs, and also the family unity in Mexico is much stronger than here in the United States, so individuals would rather place the family and God above self succession on the priority list. Traditional Mexican values places the family as the most beneficial possession one can have and if utilized properly the family's love, support, and stability can only be positive. I learned this from my grandfather, Casy Hernandez, who in 1954 immigrated to the U.S. ...

I consider myself to be just as much American as I am Hispanic, but upon growing up I encountered many discrimi-

41

nations and prejudice in American society. I have been called spic, wetback, coconut (brown on the outside, white in the middle), and many other unmentionable titles, but this name calling has never bothered me, rather the fact that America is so uneducated and immature with respect to establishing minority groups. This country is a land made up of minorities and people should be treated equally. It is not until America is wakened and educated will this country be able to spread its wings and soar to its potential height, but until then we still have the Mexicans to blame.

Ana describes the dilemma of standing between two cultures: the young Mexican-American is "like the bridge between two cultures" — the connection between the Mexican culture she experiences at home and the American culture she is often part of as a student.

Born of immigrant parents, the young Mexican-American is like the young goat who, along with her parents, lives on a pasture and is allowed to view other pastures from a bridge that connects them, but never permitted to cross it alone.

As she reaches maturity, she will finally have to cross the bridge connecting the greener pastures. The young Chicana is very much like that little goat, except she is the bridge between two cultures ... The pasture prohibited to the young goat represents the Chicana's life outside the home as a child. Earlier her social experiences are in the home, or with other Chicanos from the 'barrio', or at an occasional neighborhood piñata. The American experience is usually only at school with other children or when she accompanies her mother into town. These are like the two pastures on either side of the bridge. Once the Chicana is grown and expected to work as a professional, she experiences the once-strange culture more often. She has to cross that bridge often and meet with Anglo-American more frequently.

When I came to UCSB, I experienced this transition, and thought that I didn't fit in. It wasn't as if I had entered the room of working Anglo-American women, but I had arrived to a place where I would have to form new relationships ... It wasn't until I had an anthropology class that I realized that I could be happy with my new friends. I learned that I could remain the person that I was to satisfy my interest in my culture and at the same time I could learn to be part of a new culture to satisfy my need for others. I am glad I wasn't forced to be part of this culture because I might have lost important parts of my personal background, but I am also glad I was able to adapt to it slowly so that I could be culturally flexible enough to fit into the two cultures that are part of my interests.

Adriana examines the suffering engendered by the cycle of ethnicity, stereotypes, and discrimination:

Heredity is predetermined at birth by the parents of a child; therefore, this ethnicity cannot be changed. Being an ethnic minority in America can be a disadvantage for it may include major differences in lifestyle, beliefs, and most visible, the physical appearance of an individual compared to the 'acceptable appearance' of the Caucasian culture: white, blonde, and blue-eyed. Throughout history, most ethnic minorities ... have been stereotyped as poor, uneducated, nasty ... These assumptions about minorities help in promoting discrimination: for example, the stereotype that Asians are not assertive has led to discrepancy in job leadership positions ...

Finally, in an essay entitled "Bricks and Leggos," Elisa makes the observation that our study of cultural roots has promoted understanding and acceptance of diversity:

The American society of the twentieth century is a melting pot of many cultures. When these cultures come in conflict with each other difficulties arise in the areas of morals, customs,

43

and traditions. A conflict that resulted in segregation and racism occurred recently in Los Angeles between the Korean and Black communities. In this incident, a Korean store owner fearing that his store would be robbed shot a black teenager. Racial tensions have been mounting between these two cultures, and still no justified explanation of why it happened. Each of these communities have shown blatant racism toward each other, which seems to be spreading to the surrounding communities. The results of these type of conflicts begins to form into ethnocentrisism; seeing your culture dominant in your own eyes.

A way to combat ethocentrisism is to uncover the commonalities that bridge other cultures together. This can be done through the exploration of society's individual heritages. It begins with the ability to recognize your own heritage, what gives you your individuality. Through examining the origins of '... family stories, art, decoration, style of dress, food and all sort of daily practices ...' a person starts to uncover their true heritage.

This essay asks students to find their own focus to a greater extent than any of the previous essays, requiring them to find out what they think, how they arrived at what they think, and to communicate that process to the reader. This essay is the capstone for the course, for it encompasses all that has come before it: readings, journal writings, writing skills, and essays. Students climb Bloom's Taxonomy, from knowledge and comprehension to analysis, synthesis, and evaluation. They ascend Bloom's Scale of Intellectual Discourse, from recording "What is happening" and reporting "What happened" to generalizing about "What happens" and speculating about "What might happen." And in terms of Moffett's paradigm, students are ready to "Think Through" an idea independently, and they are able to write a thesis essay successfully

Excerpts from Diem's essay, "Bridge to Mainstream USA," exemplify this level of thinking and of writing skill.

Americans today are not only descendants of courageous Pilgrims who crossed the rough waters of the Atlantic on the Mayflower hundreds of years ago from the Old World. For many other Americans came on different boats or later, on planes, across the globe from distant lands of Africa to Asia. As a result, Americans are of every creed, social class and cultural background. Our country brings together such different peoples, the cultural medley bridged together by the varying heritage of continents. However, as the many generations of immigrants flock to their beacon of dreams, aglow with hope and opportunity, they discover that the bridge connecting to American society cannot be built merely overnight. For in every construction, stability cannot be achieved in one step.

The same weakness exists when immigrants impatiently set their foundation and realize that the bridge which they'd like to cross in order to fully assimilate into American society remains little more than a wooden frame for an initial period of time. Within this period of time, immigrants experience culture shock as they enviously see other citizens who have integrated successfully into society reap the bounty of America while their own bridge stands forlorn, unconnected to the larger framework of bustling, productive, American life. Likewise, this cultural shock which new immigrants to America experience as they struggle to assimilate into fast paced American society is addressed in Lee Ki Chuck's piece, 'From Korea to Heaven Country' where the afflictions of a young Korean immigrant was caused by his whole-hearted desire to become instantaneously American.

From the outset, the young Korean man expressed his optimism towards integrating into a society where citizens 'are always having a good time' by noting, 'Before I was Oriental guy, right? But different society ... everything is different ... like girlfriend and study and spending money and riding car.'

45

Indeed, the speaker, like immigrants who wish to be immediately American, hung around with American friends, going to rock concerts, drinking and car racing on his Pinto. He was having such a good time being American, and 'Found a lot of crazy.' All of this 'crazy' which the young immigrant found tore him apart emotionally when his hopes of success fell as his grades plummeted, disappointing his parents' bright hopes when they joined him in America ...

The result of this young man's rash behavior, took its toll when the speaker 'tried suicide.' The twenty sleeping pills luckily did not kill him, but they did kill his nonchalant attitude towards his self worth as a Korean and taught him his first major lesson on new American soil: even in fabled America, 'You have to make heaven.'

The 'terrible time' the speaker in Chuck's piece mentioned about his immigration can be spoken of by the many waves of people who laid their first stakes on American soil. For the same story can also be told by many other immigrants who yearn for a new life of freedom and opportunity and soon come to know of a less glamorous United States.

PHASE V: Pulling it All Together

Reflective writing is an essential part of metacognition—a skill students desperately need, yet get little opportunity to practice. Education must be more than learning facts. As students examine their learning processes, they will become more effective and more successful in that learning. For that reason, my students read their whole term's work: journal entries, writing exercises, research projects, and formal essays. As they read, they think not only about the subject of heritage but also about how their own thinking and writing processes have developed during this sequence. And as they read their work they write, either freewriting or listing recurrent themes or commanding entries or ideas.

> Final Journal Entry/Learning Log:
> What do I now know that I didn't before? How did I get to this point of understanding, experience? Consider what you wrote in your four previous essays and your thinking as you wrote them. How has your writing process evolved?

Some students find these topics meaningful: 1) tracing the development of critical reading skills, 2) tracing improvement in writing skills, 3) the experience of keeping a journal, 4) looking again at certain readings, 5) their appreciation for having been given the chance to evolve in their understanding and enjoyment of reading and writing, and 6) gaining an increased understanding of the cultural values and traditions of others. All these topics involve a synthesis of material and a thinking through of the writing process as well as of the subject of cultural identity.

Literature plays an enormous role in making people aware of the complications and trivialities life has to offer. Literature is a message from the writer to the reader, saying 'You aren't alone. You are not the only one who has suffered. You are not the only one who has loved.' Readers will hopefully think about the ideas conveyed in literature and become more sensitive to the lives of their fellow humans, realizing that they are indeed traveling the exact same road, a bumpy one at that. Any novel, short story, article, myth, which teaches me about life will have meaning to me. If life is what I am here for, I want to do my best.

One fact I learned this quarter is that heritage is much more complicated than the blood that flows inside each of us. Every single experience we have is affected by our heritage; where we live, what we eat, how we eat, which religion we practice, which traditions and customs we follow, even the people we encounter. Because we all have different heritages, each of us has different experiences. Luckily we all have many things in common as well. By mapping out the characters from the stories we read as insiders and outsiders to the different groups, I realized that everyone has differences and commonalties. Our lives are woven together into one perfect tapestry, colorful and grandiose in size. We are all part of this complicated tapestry called life. In many ways the Native American belief holds true; they call the plants and the animals their sisters and brothers. After earth struggling to survive. That is what we have in common — that is what we should realize.
— Kirsten

This sequence meets my teaching objectives and goals. Students gain confidence in themselves as members of the university community; they express their individual identities, at the same time interacting with others who have very different backgrounds; they learn to write in a variety of modes, moving from personal writing to source-based writing to thesis essay. They practice using writing as a way to learn, as a way to think, as a way to get more out of what they read, and as a way to express what they think and know. Diem, for example, has learned to read critically and to respond in oral and written discourse, to analyze a text, to collaborate with classmates, to write in-class timed writings, and to multi-draft formal essay assignments. Building on this knowledge, she has also learned to argue her point of view, to research a topic using library sources, to synthesize ideas from multiple sources, and to assume more responsibility for reflecting on, editing, and assessing her own writing. These goals are achieved not only through the exploration of a subject that belongs to the students, but also through the careful sequencing of assignments so success occurs. Diem and other students have been able to add skills systematically, to build momentum in their learning processes, and to find ways of making connections between texts, ideas, and skills. This continuity in English helps students see more clearly the ways in which the subject matters and skills taught in all their university classes fit together to create an education.

WHY HERITAGE?

In the multicultural writing classroom, writing problems are "also social and political problems," as David Bartholomae states in his chapter "Inventing the University" (*When a Writer Can't Write,* ed. Mike Rose, Guilford Press, 1985, p. 143). Every day I try to teach my students ways to enter the academic structure, seemingly impenetrable, which looms before them, for students must "write their way into the university" (p. 147). In order to "invent" themselves as university students, they must learn the appropriate discourse for the academy. While the task of inventing themselves is a matter of several years of education, freshman composition taught as a writing sequence can launch students on their way to building the academic skills and self-confidence they need to progress from academic "outsiders" to privileged "insiders" of the university community. Because they are experts in their subject, it allows me to learn from them; they have something to tell me that I don't know. This helps to "transform the political and social relationship" between my students and myself.

This writing sequence fulfills the needs of students (as outlined by Larson, Moffett, Bartholomae, and others) for purpose, authority, and academic skills. The good writing skills learned are applicable and transferable to all disciplines. While I am not teaching a history class, learning to write like a historian is learning to think critically, to synthesize material, and to express one's own ideas. As Bartholomae points out:

There is, to be sure, an important distinction to be made between learning history, say, and learning to write as an historian. A student can learn to command and reproduce a set of names, dates, places, and canonical interpretations (to 'tell' somebody else's knowledge); but this is not the same thing as learning to 'think' (by learning to write) as an historian. The former requires efforts of memory; the latter requires a student to compose a text out of the texts that represent the primary materials of history and in accordance with the texts that define history as an act of report and interpretation (p. 145).

I agree wholeheartedly with Bartholomae when he says that "education has failed to involve students in scholarly projects, projects that allow students to act as though they were colleagues in an academic enterprise" (p. 144). Although we often tell our students, with utter conviction, that writing is a tool for learning, in their real world experience it is often no more than a way for the university to test students' powers of reporting and summarizing.

Through writing assignment sequences and a topic that they own, my students come to see writing as a tool for learning — something they can use rather than something that can be used against them. My students see writing as more than an academic hoop they must jump through in order to get to the next obstacle.

When students share their writings with classmates, they are exposed to different ways of thinking about the topic and the readings. Their cultural biases, as well as mine, are challenged, and, at the end of the term, students point to this comparative study as one of the more valuable aspects of the course. Even those who began by saying they had no heritage discovered, by comparing their backgrounds with that of others, that there were indeed different and special things about them and their family struggles, their culture and their background.

Richard Larson suggests in his article, "Teaching Before We Judge" (*The Writing Teacher's Sourcebook*, Oxford University Press 1981, p. 208-219), that an assignment should not merely produce an essay to be judged, but should also teach by giving students an experience in reading, writing, and critical thinking. The sequential essay assignment is, as Larson describes it, like a "staircase to be climbed so that at the end the student stands higher, and has a broader prospect beneath him, than when he began. The goal of each assignment in a true sequence should be to enlarge the student's powers of thinking, organizing, and expressing ideas so that he can cope with a more complex, more challenging problem in the next assignment" (p. 212).

In addition, as Larson rightly points out, the sequencing of assignments may help students "to use their minds more effectively and to organize more successfully their experiences in the world" (p. 219). As the students move back and forth between reading and writing, they have an opportunity to engage actively in what they read. Sequencing is a powerful way to demonstrate to students that writing is a tool for learning— particularly in the close and critical reading of texts crucial to academic success.

Some Questions and Concerns

I have presented this writing sequence to various groups of of middle school, high school and college teachers. The feedback from those to whom I have spoken as well as from those who have taken my sequence into their own classrooms has pointed out their concerns and produced common questions.

Are the writing assignments too personal?

When they enter my freshman composition course, many students have written only in response to literature. They have not had experience in writing a personal essay that is the thinking through of an idea. Those who have written personal stories may not have had the opportunity to extend their own stories into more universal concepts, to make connections with the experiences and ideas of others through reading and research. This sequence combines both the personal story and the transpersonal "idea" piece. The fusion of these two forms makes the course unique and thorough in its reading and writing assignments. For the most part, students understand that all writing is personal and that the way to succeed in a writing task is, in fact, to make it personal.

*I think the writing we are doing is personal and academic. It's
a journey where we are set on a mission to explore and learn
the knowledge of one another's past and culture. It's academic because we are learning from our differences.*

— Sandra

*It's personal but we can make it as personal as we want it to
be. We can go on and talk about emotions ... and how we are
affected by these issues but we can also make it more general
and speak of our people as a group and not individuals.*

— Susana

Most of my students in the past three years have responded with
excitement to the idea of studying heritage — their own as well as that of
others.

*I was excited when I found out that the class was going to be
on Heritage. The reason being that I was always intrigued
[by] my early ancestors and their reasons for coming.* — Luz
Elena

*I thought that it was a good topic because the U.S. in reality
is composed of a mixture of all the different cultures, it is so
diverse. However, often for most of us Americans, we identify
with a culture that's more specific, for example, I identify with
my Vietnamese culture. This topic is a good way to critically
think about the culture that has influenced and caused me to
be who I am.* — Tanya

Those who were less enthusiastic were mainly concerned that they
would have nothing to write about — a common fear with any topic.
However, nearly all are positive about the theme by the middle of the
course.

*The first thing that came to my mind was 'oh my God what am
I going to do, I know nothing about my heritage.' I was*

frightened by the thought that I was not going to be able to write this paper. But then my views changed, this became a fun essay, an essay of memories and past thoughts. An essay of something thought about but only in the back of your head, never actually confronted. — Veronica

Are the assignments sufficiently academic?

Most students can see a direct relationship to other courses they must take such as history, sociology, psychology, anthropology, ethnic studies. In addition, the research assignment teaches skills that are needed in nearly all disciplines.

I can relate it to other classes like Chicano Studies because this kind of writing, all kind of writing is interrelated somehow, and if there is a focus, using what we've learned in English, we can apply it to other papers. — Sandra

This subject ... does relate to other academic areas such as history. Heritage is in fact a part of history that has carried on till today. — Tanya

In truth, the essays we write are only "personal" in the sense of being of interest to the writer, of being rooted in the writer's experience, using some family stories to blend with research and to develop ideas. These stories provide the concrete examples that make the research come alive.

When you told us about your grandmothers, I overcame my reluctance about my own family. I felt that if you could tell us something that affected her life, then it should be a little easier for me. If you let us know that you trust us with your personal information, then we can trust you. — Twilla

I write with my students, and when I share my heritage, my family stories, they feel confident in sharing their own. My students are encouraged and comforted by my own participation in the reading and writing assignments. And, as Susana noted above, they need only make it as personal as they wish. The writing assignments do not insist on personal revelation, for the reading and research provide ample material for developing the essays.

How does this sequence fit into the whole year's work?

The course represents ten weeks of work, or one quarter of a three quarter freshman composition series. I also teach a course on writing and reading memoir (developed from ideas presented by Dan Kirby at the 1991 South Coast Writing Project Institute). Like the heritage sequence, this course is based on James Moffett's ideas as presented in "Bridges: From Personal Writing to the Formal Essay." We begin by studying memoir as a literary genre, by reading various memoirs and analyses of this genre's requirements. Students write several short memoirs. In telling their own stories, students gain confidence in their ability to write. At the same time, the reading assignments require them to think analytically about how they are writing. Writing memoir is personal writing — in part, it is narrative — but it requires analysis as well, since students must find themes to connect various short pieces. By reading memoirs, writing their own, and developing a working definition of the genre, they move by degrees to higher levels of thinking and writing. Students examine how one author writes his or her memoir, how well it fits with our definition of the genre, how well it works for the reader, what theme or themes the author uses to connect the author's personal explorations. Students must use multiple sources to write a formal definition of the memoir genre, using examples, their own writing experiences, what others have said about it, as well as what the students have discovered and shared with each other along the way. Finally, students return to the writing of a personal memoir. After having read many memoirs and examined and defined the genre, their writing is enriched.

Similarly, in the heritage sequence, we turn from looking at the self toward the family or the group, then from the group toward how the many groups function in a diverse society.

In the spring I teach a course in research on the topic of "culture war." The curriculum springs out of our common text, *Culture Wars* by James Davison Hunter, a book that defines the culture war as the struggle to determine how and under what terms Americans will live together, and what comprises the good society.. The objective of the course is to explore this struggle as it affects higher education in general and UCSB in particular. [Note: We do not fight the culture war; we observe it.] Students research various aspects of our topic in a variety of ways, including interview, survey, field notes, the reading of campus publications, and library material. Their research and reports form the major portion and direction of class discussions. Students learn to frame appropriate questions, to go about finding answers, and to present these answers in both oral and written form.

This sequence lies between memoir and social criticism, between the entirely personal and the entirely transpersonal. These three sequences form a coherent year of reading and writing assignments that build confidence and joy in the writing process. Students discover that writing is a way to interact with reading material and with other people and a way to learn about themselves and about the world,

Designing Your Own Coat of Arms

Heraldry is not only fascinating, it's great fun. It is a romantic art that goes back to the days of the great Gothic cathedrals and knightly tournaments. You can create your own coat of arms and use it as a personal identification — on bookplates, on pillows and hangings, or even on your own banner.

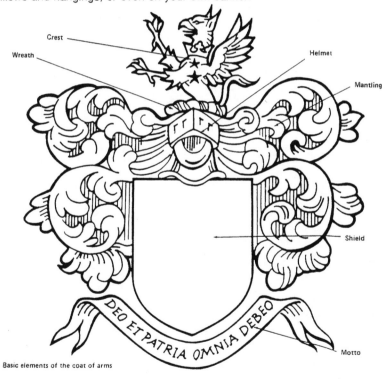

Basic elements of the coat of arms

APPENDIX B

READING ASSIGNMENTS

AN ANNOTATED BIBLIOGRAPHY

N B. In selecting the literature for my students to work with during this sequence, I have made no attempt to make my reading list "one of each," covering all possible ethnic and national groups; instead, I choose pieces according to the themes or issues they address. In this bibliography, however, I have provided a selection of literature which is about 20% each Latino, Native American, African-American, Asian-American and European; roughly half written by men, half by women.

Ardizzone, Tony. "My Mother's Stories." Beaty, p. 117-126.
The author tells the significant stories of his mother's life, including her "culturally mixed" marriage.

Baca, Jimmy Santiago. "So Mexicans Are Taking Jobs from Americans." Beaty, p. 928-929.
The poet attacks the scapegoating of a minority culture because it misdirects society's attention away from the real cause of America's difficulties.

Baldwin, James. "If Black English Isn't a Language, Then Tell Me, What Is?" DiYanni, p. 37-41.
A discussion of the social and political functions of language, and of how language is a key to both social and personal identity.

—— . "Notes of a Native Son." DiYanni, p. 52-75
An autobiographical essay that explores race relations and social issues via personal experience.

Bambara, Toni Cade. "The Lesson." Beaty, p. 931-938.
The story describes the very different values of two cultures and the difficulties of understanding the point of view of another culture.

Beaty, Jerome and J. Paul Hunter, Eds. (1989). *New worlds of literature.* **New York: W. W. Norton & Company.**
Contains a wide selection of literature from all cultures as well as a variety of genres — poetry, short fiction, essay, and drama.

Bruchac, Joseph. "Ellis Island." Beaty, p. 290.
The poet describes the immigration of his European ancestors and his conflicting feelings about how immigration has affected the fate of his Native American ancestors.

Burns, Diane. "Sure You Can Ask Me A Personal Question." Beaty, p. 578.
The poet explores the dangers, sometimes subtle and seemingly innocent, of ethnic stereotyping.

Chuck, Lee Ki. "From Korea to Heaven Country." Beaty, p. 28-31.
A transcription of an oral interview with a Korean-American that vividly describes the misconceptions about America as a "heaven" country as well as the enormous difficulties of fitting into a new culture.

Clifford, John and Robert DiYanni, Eds. (1987). *Modern American prose: 15 Writers.* **New York: Random House.**

Gogisgi. "Song of the Breed." Beaty, p. 868-869.
The poet describes his feeling of being caught between his Native American culture and the white culture.

Hogan, Linda. "Heritage." Beaty, p. 246-247.
The poet describes the different qualities, both physical and cultural, she has inherited from her Native American family.

—. "Song for My Name." Beaty, p. 508-S09
A traditional Native American "naming" song.

Hoy, Pat C. and Robert DiYanni, Eds. (1988). *Prose pieces: Essays and stories, sixteen modern writers.* **New York: Random House.**

Hunter, John Davison. (1991). *Culture wars: The struggle to define America.* **New York: Basicbooks, HarperCollins Publishers.**

Josephy, Alvin M. (1976). "Indians Today and Their Fight for Survival." *The Indian heritage of America.* **New York: Bantam Books.**
The author explodes some of American society's assumptions about the positive nature of assimilation by analyzing the choice of some Native Americans not to blend.

Kingston, Maxine Hong. "No Name Woman." Beaty, p. 299-309
The author develops the themes of traditional sexual mores, as well as unfair and punitive gender roles.

Miyasaki, Gail Y. "Obachan." Beaty, p. 261-264
The author explores the problems of marrying outside the tribe, the value of tradition, and the difficulties of assimilation.

Mora, Pat "Sonrisas. " Beaty, p. 697-698.
The poet vividly describes her position "in a doorway" between her Chicana heritage and that of the Anglo-Americans.

Okita, Dwight. "In Response to Executive Order 9066: ALL AMERI-CANS OF JAPANESE DESCENT MUST REPORT TO RELOCA-TION CENTERS." Beaty, p. 721-723.
Written from his mother's point of view as a fourteen-year-old girl, the poet describes the bewilderment and sadness of a girl ordered to leave her school and friends for life in a relocation camp.

Olivas, Richard. "I'm Sitting in My History Class." Beaty, p. 349-350.
A minority student asks about the relevance of white American history to him.

Padilla, Elena. "Migrants: Transients or Settlers?" Beaty, p. 53-S8.
The author raises difficult questions about making the choice to assimi-late into a new culture and the conflict between those who do and those who choose not to.

Pastan, Linda. "Grudnow." Beaty, p. 297-298.
The poet tells the story of her Polish grandfather's home and the effect of his immigration on her own life.

Rodriguez, Richard. "Aria: A Memoir of a Bilingual Childhood." Beaty, p. 483-500.
The author explains his choice to abandon his native language and adopt English as an avenue to social and political power and acceptance.

Rushin, Donna Kate. "The Bridge Poem." Beaty, p. 694-696.
The poet expresses disgust with her role as a token African-American, a bridge between various groups who claim her and expect her to act as a go-between, explaining one group to another.

Schwartz, Rhoda. "Old Photographs." Beaty, p. 138-140.
The poet describes her Russian heritage through a series of "photo-graphs."

Soto, Gary. "Like Mexicans." Beaty, p. 817-820.
The author tells the story of his decision to marry outside his Mexican heritage and how he discovered that the Japanese woman he loved and her family were "just like Mexicans."

Tuchman, Barbara. "In Search of History." DiYanni, p. 395-402.
An essay about the historian's writing process, sources and methods for research, and about the purposes of writing history.

Walker, Alice. "Everyday Use." Hoy, p. 535-542.
The author raises questions about the definition of heritage, the value of family heirlooms, of traditions, and of family pride.

—-. "In Search of Our Mothers' Gardens." DiYanni, p. 451-462.
The author pays tribute to her ancestors, poor black women, who found ways to express their creativity in spite of oppression and poverty.

APPENDIX C

LIBRARY RESOURCES

Allen, H. G.. (1890). *The Encyclopedia Britannica: A dictionary of arts, sciences and general literature.* (9th ed.). New York.

Barton, M. with contributions from Cashmore, E., [et. al.] (1984). *Dictionary of race and ethnic relations.* London; Boston: Routledge & Kegan Paul.

Bernard, G. (c.1991). *The timetables of history: A horizontal linkage of people and events* (new 3rd rev. ed.). New York: Simon and Schuster.

Fischel, J. & Pinsker, S. (Eds.). (1992). *Jewish-American history and culture: An encyclopedia.* New York: Garland reference library of social science; v. 429.

Grolier, C., (1992). *Encyclopedia Americana* (International ed.). Danbury, Connecticut.

Handlin, O., Orlov, A., & Thernstrom, S. (Eds.). (1980). *The Harvard encyclopedia of American ethnic groups.* Cambridge, MA: Belknap Press of Harvard University.

Kim, Hyung-Chan (Ed.) (1986). *Dictionary of Asian American history.* New York: Greenwood Press.

Langer, W. (compiled and edited). (1975). *The new illustrated encyclopedia of world history,* Volumes 1 & 2 (1st ed.). New York: H.N. Abrams.

Meier, Matt S. and Rivera, F. (1981). *Dictionary of Mexican American history.* Westport, Conn.: Greenwood Press.

Ploski, H. A. & Williams, J. (compiled and edited). (1990). *Reference library of black America.* Detroit, MI: Gale Research, Inc.; distributed by Afro American Press.

The Random House timetables of history. (1991). New York, NY: Random House.

Steinberg, S.H.; forward by Gooch, G.P.; updated by Paxton, J. (c.1986). *Historical tables, 58 B.C. - A.D. 1985* (11th ed.). New York: Garland Pub.

Trager, J. (ed.). (c.1992). *The people's chronology: A year-by-year record of human events from pre-history to the present* (revised and updated ed.). New York: Holt, H.

APPENDIX D

ADDITIONAL READINGS

Angelou, Maya. (1969). *I know why the caged bird sings.* New York: Random House, Inc.

Baca, Jimmy Santiago. (1979). *Immigrants in our own land.* Baton Rouge: Louisiana State University Press.

Bache, Ellyn. (1989). *Culture clash.* Yarmouth, ME: Intercultural Press, Inc.

Baldwin, James. (1984). *Notes of a native son.* Boston: Beacon Press.

Carter, Forrest. (1991). *The education of Little Tree.* Albuquerque: University of New Mexico Press.

Cisneros, Sandra. (1991). *The house on Mango Street.* New York: Vintage Books, Random House, Inc.

Dillard, Annie. (1987). *An American childhood.* New York: Harper & Row.

Kingston, Maxine Hong. *(1976). The woman warrior: Memoirs of a girlhood among ghosts.* New York: Alfred A. Knopf. distributed by Random House.

Momaday, Scott. (1969).*The way to Rainy Mountain.* Albuquerque: University of New Mexico Press.

Momaday, Scott. (1976). *The names: A memoir.* New York: Harper & Row.

Namias, June, ed. (1978). *First generation: In the words of twentieth century American immigrants.* Boston: Beacon Press.

Rodriguez, Richard. (1981). *Hunger of memory: The education of Richard Rodriguez.* Boston, MA: D.R. Godine.

Salzman, Mark. (1986). *Iron and silk.* New York: Random House.

Song, Cathy. (1988). *Frameless windows, squares of light: Poems by Cathy Song.* New York: W.W. Norton and Company, Inc.

Soto, Gary. (1985). *Living up the street: Narrative recollections.* San Francisco, CA: Strawberry Hill Press.

Tan, Amy. (1989). *The Joy Luck Club.* New York: Ivy Books, Ballantine Books.

Thomas, Joyce Carol, ed. (1990). *A gathering of flowers: Stories about being young in America.* New York: Harper Keypoint, Harper Collins Publishers.

Walker, Alice. (1973). *In love and trouble: Stories of black women.* New York: Harcourt Brace Jovanovich, Inc.

Wright, Richard. (1945). *Black boy: A record of childhood and youth.* New York: Harper Collins Publishers.

APPENDIX E

GRADING RUBRIC

A (SUPERIOR) An "A" paper commands attention because of its insightful, cogent response to the assignment. Reasoning is persuasive and supported by detailed, relevant examples. The central point is focused for a specific audience, clearly defined, and gracefully stated. Organizational strategies are coherent, well-chosen, and consistently controlled. Paragraph breaks correspond to shifts in topic; paragraph topics are focused and clearly articulated; transitions are smooth and logical. Original imagery is used to convey thoughts and emotions. Ideas are expressed clearly, directly, and concisely; sentences are consistently well-constructed; style is sophisticated and varied, showing an awareness of rhetorical and stylistic options. Research is thorough, well documented, and effectively integrated into the text. Final draft is close to error-free.

B (GOOD) A "B" paper provides a thoughtful, well-developed response to the assignment. Reasoning is sensible and supported by appropriate examples. The central idea is focused and clearly defined. Organization strategies are coherent and controlled. Paragraph breaks correspond to shifts in topic. The paragraph topics are usually focused. Transitions are attempted although sometimes weak or ineffective. Imagery is unoriginal and ineffective. Ideas are usually expressed clearly but the prose is characterized by a lack of directness and/or conciseness; frequently imprecise word choice; little sentence variety; occasional major errors in grammar/frequent minor errors. There is evidence of research, but it is not always appropriately used or effectively integrated into the text.

71

C (FAIR) A "C" paper presents an adequate response to the assignment and develops that response with acceptable reasoning and adequate examples, but these examples are sometimes sketchy, vague or repetitious. The thesis or central point is apparent but not clearly stated. Organizational strategies are usually controlled. Paragraph breaks usually correspond to shifts in topic. The paragraph topics are usually focused. Transitions are attempted although sometimes weak or ineffective. Imagery is unoriginal and ineffective. Ideas are usually expressed clearly but the prose is characterized by a lack of directness and/or conciseness; frequently imprecise word choice; little sentence variety; occasional major errors in grammar and frequent minor errors. There is evidence of research, but it is not always appropriately used or effectively integrated into the text.

D (POOR) A "D" paper responds to the assignment in an illogical and incomplete way. While some good examples are provided, for the most part the essay is underdeveloped. The central point is confusing, sometimes contradictory, and not explicitly stated. Organizational strategies are only partially in control and applied inconsistently. Paragraph breaks are arbitrary and paragraph topics are not always apparent. Transitions are choppy. Ideas are often obscured by repeated major errors in grammar and usage. Little evidence of research, and that is poorly documented and ineffectively used to develop the paper.

F (UNACCEPTABLE) An "F" paper presents a simplistic, inappropriate and/or incoherent response to the assignment. The central point is not apparent and it is inappropriately brief. Organizational strategies are not apparent. Ideas are obscured by repeated major errors in grammar and usage. No research evident.

ABOUT THE AUTHOR

Deborah Dixon is a lecturer at the University of California, Santa Barbara, and a part-time instructor at Moorpark College, Moorpark, California. She is a teacher consultant with the South Coast Writing Project.

She teaches ballet at a local dance studio, and enjoys mysteries (Sue Grafton) and science fiction (Anne McCaffrey). Once a month she meets with her writing group, four women who are also South Coast Writing Project fellows, to write and share writing as well as to discuss teaching.